LAO T...

TAO
TE CHING

Chinese Popular Classics

This new and innovative Chinese Popular Classics series will take you to the heart of the Chinese world. One quarter of the world's population is Chinese, yet the great and ancient culture of China is barely known in the West. This is especially true of the popular beliefs which have shaped folk religion and culture in China for over 2000 years. These beliefs offer insights and understanding of relevance for the wider world and are increasingly being recognised as significant religious and spiritual teachings. What was in the past often dismissed by the scornful West as superstition or peasant lore, is now seen to reflect centuries of wisdom.

The team behind the series comes from the International Consultancy on Religion, Education and Culture (ICOREC) who for over twelve years have led the way in translating Chinese religious texts. It is headed by Martin Palmer, whose translations of Chinese texts have established him as one of the foremost interpreters of Chinese folk religion in the UK today. The team brings together Taoist priests, monks, organisations such as the China Taoist Association, feng shui masters, scholars of classical Chinese, poets and researchers, both in the UK and in China. With their assistance it is possible to explore the mythological and philosophical, practical and mystical worlds of popular Chinese culture.

To understand China you need to understand her soul. Through this series, such a journey of exploration can begin.

CHINESE
POPULAR CLASSICS

LAO TZU'S
TAO
TE CHING

A NEW VERSION BY
TIMOTHY FREKE

SERIES EDITOR
MARTIN PALMER

PIATKUS

The cover embroidery is a detail from a Chinese silk tapestry of the Wanli period (1573–1619). It has a background of gold thread and is decorated with lotus flowers and leafy stems. Featured on the tapestry are two dragons chasing flaming pearls through the clouds. Among the dragons are double gourds and canopies which were used as decoration for the New Year Festival and Lantern Festival, which were ten days apart in the Chinese calender. The tapestry is reproduced courtesy of Spink and Son Ltd, London.

All the illustrations and Chinese characters used in the book are the copyright of Circa Photo Library.

© 1995 ICOREC

First published in 1995 by
Judy Piatkus (Publishers) Ltd
5 Windmill Street, London W1P 1HF

A catalogue record for this book is available from the British Library

ISBN 0-7499-1468-8

Designed by Zena Flax

Typeset in Galliard
Data capture and manipulation by
Action Typesetting Ltd, Gloucester

Printed & bound in Great Britain by
Biddles Ltd, Guildford & King's Lynn

Contents

知

Acknowledgements

Love and thanks to Victoria Moseley for reading and rereading this rendering – helping me hone and refine it. Respect and gratitude to Martin Palmer for editing this work, and to Susan Mears for acting as my agent. Also to Ram Dass, whose insight, humour and humanity have profoundly influenced the way I see life, and therefore the way I have interpreted this text. Finally eternal gratitude to my father and mother, without whose continuing love and support I would never have found the time and opportunity to explore spirituality and creativity in the way I have been able to.

Timothy Freke

Introduction

The *Tao Te Ching* is now acknowledged as one of the great spiritual and philosophical classics of the world. It speaks directly and simply of a world of order that we must work with, not of a chaotic world where we must just fend for ourselves. Described as a manual of leadership, it is also a classic of meditation. It is for these reasons and for many more that the book has become as revered as it is today. But what exactly is this book? Where did it come from, and why does it speak to us so powerfully today?

Its title means the Classic (*Ching*) of the Way (*Tao*) and Virtue (*Te*), and it is also known as the *Lao Tzu*, after its supposed author. The terms *Tao* and *Te* are central ideas in Chinese philosophy which emerged in the extraordinary flourishing of new thought between the sixth and fourth centuries BC. Yet the title tells us very little about the book; for this we need to look deeper into the meaning of Tao.

You might expect a Taoist text to have been written by a Taoist, but this is not the case. The term Taoist as a description of a specific group only begins to be used about 100 BC. Lao Tzu, or whoever it was who compiled this book, was not a Taoist. He, or even possibly she, was a thinker, a philosopher, who explored the depths of the concept of the Tao. But this was also done by others who have nothing to do with what we now call Taoism (see pages 23–5). For example, Confucius (K'ung Fu Tzu) wrote extensively on the Tao, but he is not described today as a Taoist.

The concept of Tao – the Way – was one which the thinkers of the past used to cover many areas of what we would today call spirituality, religion, ethics and morality. In the *Tao Te Ching* it is seen as the fundamental force or inspiration which fills all life – indeed, according to chapter 42, which brings all to life. The text goes even further, describing the Tao as that which gives birth to the Origin. It thus becomes the force behind and beyond all forces. But it is not a divine force; it is simply yet gloriously the ultimate expression or origin of all that is natural. Hence the emphasis throughout the book on following the natural path, of flowing with nature and not trying to impose humanity's puny will against the reality of nature.

Tao and Te

The word 'Tao' is a very simple one in Chinese. It means 'road' or 'path'. Look at any directory of a Chinese city such as Shanghai or Hong Kong and you will hundreds if not thousands of Taos – Central Tao, Beijing Tao and so on. The character combines the radical or base character for 'walk' with the radical character for 'head'. Combined, it means to walk ahead, to go ahead, to travel to the end: in other words, to take a road or path.

The word, however, soon began to acquire a much deeper meaning. For example, by the ninth or eighth centuries BC it was already being used in two very different ways. In the first of these it had ethical or moral connotations, especially where fate or destiny was understood to be a road or path from which one could not deviate. In the Councils of the Mighty Yu, contained within the *Book of*

History (Shu Ching), one of the five Confucianist classics which was written in this period, the words are found: 'I see how great is your virtue, how admirable your vast achievements. The specific choice of Heaven rests upon you: you must eventually take the throne of the great ruler. The mind of humanity is restless and likely to fail; its willingness to follow the Tao is small.' (*Shu Ching*, Part II) Here the Emperor Shun is talking to one of the great moral and physical heroes of ancient China, Yu, who had tamed the raging Yellow River. He is being told that it is right and proper, the Tao, that he should ascend the throne, and not an act of rebellion or treason, for this is what the Tao wants. If Yu does as he is destined, then the Tao will be manifested. If he refuses, then he is acting like a small-minded person who does not comprehend their position within the greater scheme of things – the Tao.

The second meaning of the Tao is the Way of Heaven. In many sections of the *Tao Te Ching* the text puts the character for Heaven together with that of Tao, Heaven's Tao or the Tao of Heaven. Let's look at another text from the *Shu Ching*. This time, the Tao is more than just a moral code; it is an eternal verity, a way which courses through time and across the universe and which will carry you with it or drop you if you fight against it. It is beginning to approach the Tao of the *Tao Te Ching*:

> I have heard the saying: 'He who finds himself teachers, will rule the greatest area; he who says no one is his equal, will fall. He who is willing to ask, becomes greater; he who relies entirely upon himself, will be humbled and made small'. So, he who wishes to be sure of his end, must look to his beginning. There is security for those who observe propriety and disaster for those who are blind and

pay no attention. To revere and honour the Tao of
Heaven is the way to ensure the favour of Heaven
for ever. (*Shu Ching*, Part IV)

So by the time Confucius and Lao Tzu appear upon the
scene, in the sixth century BC, the term 'Tao' has begun to
have two distinct meanings. One is moralistic and concerned with virtue as an expression of an ultimate purpose
and pattern; the other, captured in the term 'Tao of
Heaven', is more cosmic and causal than moral and pre-
scriptive. In the writings of Confucius these two aspects
are sharply defined. For example, on the moralistic, pre-
scriptive side we have this text from *The Analects* (the
major text credited to Confucius): 'The Master said, "If the
people follow the Tao because of laws and punishments,
they will certainly try to avoid punishment but will have
no sense of shame. If they follow the Tao of virtue (Te)
and are guided by rules of what it is right to do, they will
have a sense of shame and will thus become better.' (Ch. 2.
3). But Confucius also teaches a more cosmic vision of
Tao, which is very close to much within the *Tao Te Ching*:

> Confucius said: When the Tao prevails in the
> world, the rites, music and punitive military
> expeditions are initiated by the Emperor. When the
> Tao does not prevail in the world, they are initiated
> by the lesser lords.... When the Tao prevails in the
> world, policy is not in the hands of the Advisers.
> When the Tao prevails in the world, there is
> nothing for the ordinary people to argue about.
> (16.2)

By the time we get to the *Tao Te Ching*, the Tao has all
these nuances and more. For now the Tao has not just

become the Tao of Heaven, but actually subsumes Heaven within itself. It has become the ultimate principle of all existence, above, beyond, within, around and exceeding all that is. Chapter 4 captures this perfectly, for, as Timothy Freke puts it:

> Tao is like an empty space,
> that can never be filled up.
> Yet it contains everything:
> Blunt and sharp,
> resolved and confused,
> bright and dull,
> the whole of Creation.
>
> Hidden, but always present.
> Who created it?
> It existed before the Creator.

In the *Tao Te Ching* we find, for the first time in Chinese literature, the notion of the Tao as the Ultimate beyond the Ultimate, the All from which everything came. This is where the *Tao Te Ching* moves on to new territory in Chinese thought. Even the gods and spirits are just part of this Absolute Tao. This is the heart of the *Tao Te Ching* – the introduction of the Tao as the Supreme. Not, note, Supreme Being. The Tao has no personality. It is not a god or divinity. It just is what is, and as such is the Ultimate beingness of life.

But the Tao is also fused with, and balanced by, the Te, as yin balances yang. Te is usually translated as 'virtue', although the poet and oriental scholar Arthur Waley translates it as 'power', giving us the Way and its Power. 'Virtue' is perhaps a rather narrow definition of its meaning, but it does capture something of the logical outcome of following the Tao – the moral behaviour that should flow from following the Tao.

This is already present in Confucius's words quoted earlier, where the Tao and the Te together produce a sense of what is right and wrong and thus produce shame when someone acts wrongly. The Te is the outworking of the Tao, hence Waley's use of the word 'power'.

What the Te brings to the *Tao Te Ching* is consequence. Without the Te, the *Tao Te Ching* would be no more than a book of nice sayings. With the Te, it is a handbook of applied wisdom. It is no accident that the *Tao Te Ching* has spawned many books in the West which call themselves such things as the *Tao of Leadership*, the *Tao of Management*, the *Tao of Business* and so on.

The *Tao Te Ching* often talks of the 'sage', or, as Timothy has expressed it, the 'wise'. I think his phrase is a good one because the notion of the sage is of one who retreats from the world and is unworldly. Yet the wise one in the *Tao Te Ching* is frequently discussing battle plans, control of populations, mass media impact and the like. He (or she) is concerned with making people live and behave properly, but without resorting to the crudeness of violence or murder. This wise one is wise in philosophy and politics, meditation and warfare. Perhaps this is why the book has so appealed to our age, living as we do in such diverse and often competitive worlds.

The structure of the Tao Te Ching

I have touched upon the *Tao Te Ching*'s message, but the book defies easy categorisation. It consists of a series of quotes, sayings, oracles, wisdom proverbs and folklore, and if you try to read it straight through as a text you will be disappointed. There is no coherence to the *Tao Te Ching* other than the exploration of wisdom sayings through the 'editorial commentary' that follows each one, and the flow of the Tao and its consequences expressed in Te. Most chapters have little, if anything, to do with the ones that precede and follow. The book is not a developing argument or account, but a collection of isolated pearls of wisdom, strung together as on a necklace. Each one is rounded and perfect in its own right, creating together an overall impression of beauty and significance.

So do not try to 'read' the *Tao Te Ching*. Try instead to dip into it, to enjoy each chapter on its own, to find phrases which speak directly to you. And if a chapter doesn't touch you, move on, for there will come a time when it is right to reread that chapter. If you approach the book this way, you will find that it is as fresh to you as it has been to countless millions of Chinese down the centuries. Just enter the flow of its thought and world vision and allow yourself to be swept along by it.

Over the centuries, popular and familiar sayings become rounded and balanced so as to be easily remembered. Let's take an example that Jesus used in Matthew 16, verses 2–3, which in common everyday English goes:

> Red sky at night, shepherd's delight;
> Red sky at morning, shepherd's warning

The quote is easily remembered because each line contains exactly the same number of words and they mirror each other; in addition, the rhythm and rhyme make the phrases roll easily off the tongue. This is precisely what every chapter of the *Tao Te Ching* in Chinese contains, usually at the start. The rest of the text is completely different in style and consists of a commentary which unravels the meaning or points us onwards from the verse or saying.

In Timothy's wonderful new rendering this can be very clearly seen at times; although, in fairness, Timothy was not working from Chinese texts and so could be freer in his style than a translation would be. However, even in this free rendering, the pattern holds. Look at chapter 1: the first six lines are the wisdom saying while the last part is the commentary, and the change in style is quite marked. Chapter 12 offers a similarly clear example: the first five sentences are the wisdom saying and the last three sentences are commentary. In this rendering, Timothy has sought to capture the essence of the text without being caught up in the particulars of the Chinese. The result is the beautiful, flowing text you now have before you.

The origins of the book

Traditionally the book has been seen as the work of one man – Lao Tzu. The legendary account of its origin goes like this. Long ago in China, some five hundred years or so before the birth of Christ, there lived a wise man. For many years this man, one Li Erh Tan, worked as the court archivist in the state of Chou. A man of remarkable philosophical skill and insight, he had become disgusted by the decline in standards and wisdom in his state and so resigned his post and departed for the West. After a long journey he reached the edge of the Chinese world, at the mountain pass known as Han Ku, where he stopped for the night. The gatekeeper, Kuan Yin, sat and talked with his distinguished visitor and was amazed at the wisdom, learning and teachings of this elderly man, known by his honorific title of Old Master – Lao Tzu. Kuan Yin begged Lao Tzu to leave behind him one text which would encapsulate all his teachings. Lao Tzu obliged, and in the course of that one night he wrote a five thousand-word book which we now know as the *Tao Te Ching*. As the morning light rose above the mountains, Lao Tzu placed the text in the hands of Kuan Yin and went out through the pass. He was never seen again.

In fact the term 'go West' in Chinese is a euphemism for death. West, in classical Chinese thought, is the direction of Paradise, in just the same way as the East has always been for Westerners. So when tradition says that Lao Tzu went West, what is being spoken of is his death. In this setting, the gatekeeper of the pass is none other than Death, or, in Chinese thought, one of the creatures who came to collect the soul.

The real story of the *Tao Te Ching* is a little more complex. It was not written in one night but took shape over some seven or eight hundred years. It was not written on the edge of the Chinese world, but almost certainly at its heart. Whoever the author or editor of the text was, it was not Lao Tzu.

The *Tao Te Ching* is one of the oldest texts of China. It is not as old as the *I Ching*, nor as old as many of the texts in the great *Classic of Poetry* and *Classic of History*. Yet it contains material which comes from the same period as the *I Ching*. It was compiled between the sixth and fourth centuries BC, when China witnessed the flourishing of the 'Hundred Schools' of philosophy. This was a time when sages, philosophers and charlatans wandered across China, followed by their schools of disciples, arguing about the nature of existence, the meaning of meaning and all manner of other ideas. This philosophical flowering produced great figures such as Confucius (K'ung Fu Tzu), Mencius (Meng Tzu), Chuang Tzu, Lieh Tzu and, of course, Lao Tzu. It was also a time during which much wisdom and knowledge from the earliest days of Chinese civilisation, which had been kept alive through storytelling, oral history, poetry, myths, legends and folk sayings, was committed to writing for the first time. Many of the earliest Chinese books, still extant today, were compiled in these centuries.

Divination and oracles

But we need to go a long way back before this to find the roots of the *Tao Te Ching*. We need to go to high mountains and to the priestly shamans who lived upon them. But most of all we need to go back to divination, for preserved within the *Tao Te Ching* are divinations, oracles and sayings from the earliest years of Chinese civilisation.

Shamanism can lay claim to being the oldest world religion, having begun at least eight thousand years ago in Siberia. From there it spread across the land bridge then existing between Siberia and Alaska, to North and Central America. It filtered south from Siberia into China and on beyond to Indonesia, South-east Asia and further afield. West, it reached as far as the northern tribes of Finland.

At its heart is a vision of the physical or material world as an inferior place. The superior world is the spirit world, which occasionally breaks through into this material world. The role of the shaman was to mediate between these two worlds and to invoke the assistance of the spirit world in affairs of this world such as illness, warfare and daily problems. By entering into a trance the shaman could communicate with the spirit world and through affinity with other creatures, especially bears, he or she could enter into a relationship with other species who had an almost natural affinity with the spirit world. The shamans, who could be of either sex, though women seem to have predominated in the earliest years, wielded considerable power, and their opinions – or rather the opinions of the gods and spirits which they could reveal – were sought by the powerful. It was from these shamanistic practices that Chinese as a written language, and the first elements of the text of the *Tao Te Ching*, emerged.

Some time around 2000–1700 BC a form of divination had arisen, which used either tortoise shells or ox shoulder bones. A question would be asked of the oracle bone – it might be as mundane as 'Should the king go hunting today' or as historic as 'Should the capital city be moved?' Then the shamans would make small indentations on the underside of the bone or shell. A heated stick or rod was applied to the indentation, which caused cracks to appear on the upper side of the bone or shell. These cracks were then 'read', quite literally. For example, if there were three wavy lines, this was taken to mean water; a circular shape was the sun, and so forth. In other words, the pictogram nature of the Chinese characters comes from shamans looking at cracks on bones and seeing pictures which provided the answer to a question.

When these answers proved to be particularly auspicious or significant – or possibly even true – the bones were carved with more stylised versions of the pictures and kept as royal archives. This is why tens of thousands of them have been found at each of the major centres of the Shang dynasty (*c.* 1700–1100 BC).

Hundreds of thousands of oracles were produced. Most of them were forgotten over the following centuries, but it is obvious that some found their way into a wider culture either because they expressed an insight or wisdom which transcended the particular occasion that had caused their delivery, or because they were associated with some momentous event which was celebrated for years afterwards. This is what lies behind the *I Ching*'s original oracle texts. They led the Chou tribes to rise up against the oppressive but collapsing Shang dynasty and overthrow it. Having inspired the revolt and guided its military campaign, the oracles were preserved by being recited at the annual celebration of the uprising. Other oracles passed into general circulation in a similar way. Such oracles and wise sayings are central to the structure of the *Tao Te Ching*.

The place of Lao Tzu

In chapters 20, 21, 25, 43, 49, 67 and 70, and nowhere else, the text speaks in the first person singular. I believe that this 'I' who speaks so directly to us is the original Lao Tzu. Here we have a collection of sayings from the man himself, which the editor respected so deeply that he or she did not change them into the impersonal style of the rest of the book. And here is the clue as to how the book came into being.

Originally there was obviously a collection of sayings associated with Lao Tzu. Over the years after his death this collection circulated, probably in oral form, though it is also possible that they were recorded in writing. Gradually the name Lao Tzu came to be associated with wise sayings, and other such sayings began to accrue to the collection.

Later, around the fourth century BC, someone decided to edit the various sayings and to add a commentary. We know nothing whatsoever about this person – only that she or he was a genius. The selection of sayings and the wisdom of the commentaries show a mind of quite exceptional brilliance.

So Lao Tzu, a man who deflated swollen egos and shunned office, power or any trappings of authority, was merely the spark from which this great work sprang. So why did the later editor claim that the whole *Tao Te Ching* was Lao Tzu's? The answer is very simple. It is a relatively recent phenomenon to insist upon historical accuracy for a text. In the past, if you wrote what you considered to be a good text you would honour a god or historical figure by saying it was written by them. No disrespect was meant; indeed quite the opposite. In the classic *Chuang Tzu*, the fourth century BC book named after the second sage of Taoism, there is a whole discussion about what he calls 'supposed words', words that are put into the mouths of figures of authority from the past, precisely, says the *Chuang Tzu*, so that people today will pay attention to them. Thus, in claiming that the book was entirely Lao Tzu's, the editor was trying to ensure that people who otherwise would pay no attention to it would read the book and consider it worthy of further study.

Many stories are told of the great Lao Tzu, perhaps the most famous being that of his meeting with K'ung Fu Tzu (Confucius). This is how Ssu Ma Ch'ien, China's first proper historian (*c*. 100 BC), recounts this encounter:

> When K'ung Fu Tzu went to Chou, he asked Lao
> Tzu to tutor him in the rites. Lao Tzu replied,
> 'The very bones of those you talk about have
> turned to dust. All that remains of them is their
> words. You know that when a noble lives in times
> which are good, he travels to the court by carriage.
> But when times are difficult, he goes where the
> wind blows. Some say a wise merchant hides his
> wealth and thus seems poor. Likewise the sage, if
> he has great internal virtue, seems on the outside
> to be a fool. Stop being so arrogant; all these
> demands; your self-importance and over-keen
> enthusiasm – none of this is true to yourself. That
> is all I have to say to you.'
>
> Kung left and said to his followers, 'I know that

a bird can fly; that fishes swim; that animals can run. Things that run can be trapped in nets. What can swim can be caught in traps. Those that fly can be shot down with arrows. But what to do with the dragon I do not know. It rises on the clouds and the wind. Today I have met Lao Tzu and he is like the dragon.'

This is a classic piece of Taoist narrative, capturing the sharp tongue of the Taoist sage who uses brief sermons full of allusions to silence the fools of this world! Similar accounts of Lao Tzu's words and actions can be found in Chuang Tzu, often in connection with further encounters with K'ung Fu Tzu.

Down the centuries Lao Tzu's wisdom has been developed and reinterpreted in various ways. When the Buddhists began to make major inroads into China in the fourth to eighth centuries AD, the Taoists were at first very displeased. Then they recalled that Lao Tzu had lived around the same time as the Buddha, in about the fifth or sixth century BC. He had then disappeared 'into the West'. So, said the Taoists, obviously Lao Tzu had travelled to India where he had taught. One of his promising pupils was a rich young man called Siddhartha Gautama. Unfortunately, he was rather an arrogant young man and, having grasped only a fraction of Lao Tzu's wisdom, he rushed off and, using these garbled versions of his master's teachings, set up a religion all of his own. Yes, said the Taoists, the Buddha was a not very successful student of Lao Tzu!

But a more interesting transformation has taken place for Lao Tzu. The philosopher sage has become a god; and not just any god, but one of the three great Taoist deities whose existence pre-dates all creation and who will live for ever. In most Taoist temples around the world Lao Tzu is venerated and worshipped, his assistance invoked for everything from marital harmony through sickness to success in exams. For around the figure of Lao Tzu a vast and complex faith has grown up whose key text is the *Tao Te Ching*, but used in a way which would startle most Westerns who think they know what the book is about. For the world of Taoism is one of magic, divination, gods and spirits. It seems a million miles away from the philosophy of the Tao and of the insights of the Tao Te Ching. Yet they are linked in a very vital way.

But before we look at Taoism as a religion, let's look more closely at what happened to the book itself.

A chequered history

The book traditionally divides into two sections: the first, chapters 1 to 37, named Tao, and the second, chapter 38 to the end, named Te. Yet the earliest copy of the text that we have, from a tomb dated 168 BC, has the two sections the other way round. The *Tao Te Ching* was originally written on strips of bamboo, which were strung together side by side to make a book. No clear numbering system for chapters seems to have been used, and so the order of the text relied upon tradition and copying older versions. This was fine until the dreadful year 213 BC.

In 221 BC, a mighty warrior king conquered the last remaining independent kingdom in China. Indeed, so powerful was he and so immense his impact that our own word 'China' comes from the name of his all-victorious kingdom of Ch'in. This king, Ch'in Shi Huang Ti, was brutal beyond belief and his path to victory lay over mounds of dead. Like other megalomaniacs, he believed he was establishing a dynasty which would rule for thousands of years. In 213 BC, he ordered the burning of all books except those on medicine, divination and agriculture. His intention was simple. By destroying all records of previous times, other ways of thinking and other ways of ruling, no one would realise that things could be different. Innumerable copies of the great texts were destroyed. Confucian scholars who resisted were buried alive. Libraries were burnt to the ground. It was a terrible time for China.

But many texts were hidden. For example, in Qufu, the home town of K'ung Fu Tzu, you can still see the site of the wall into which his texts were plastered to hide them, not to be rediscovered for many years. All over China similar action was taken. Amongst the texts designed to be wiped out for ever by this Burning of the Books, some two thousand years before Hitler, was the *Tao Te Ching*. Its philosophy and advice to rulers ran totally contrary to the new dictatorship, so any copies which survived did so by being hidden.

In the damp of hiding places the cords of the bamboo books rotted and, when the texts were recovered, they would have been in a complete muddle. Chinese scholarship has spent considerable time trying to work out which lines originally went where. In my own translation of the *Tao Te Ching* (Kwok, Palmer and Ramsay, Element Books 1993) we have followed modern Chinese scholarship and considerably altered the arrangement of certain chapters. In this rendering, Timothy has followed the traditional arrangement. However he felt uneasy about three chapters and suggested that parts of them belonged elsewhere. Therefore, following joint research, he has placed parts of chapter 42 in 39, parts of 29 in 64 and, by adding the part from 42 to 39, has changed the layout of that chapter to indicate two different sections within the one chapter. Otherwise, readers will find here a text that by and large follows the traditional arrangement.

We do not know what the original title of the book was.

The earliest reference is by the third-century BC writer Han Fei Tzu, who calls it the *Tè Tao* – reflecting the reversed order found in the oldest extant copy. The word *Ching* (Classic) was not added until the Han period (207 BC–AD 220), when Taoism began to emerge as a distinct religion. In fact the inclusion of the word *Ching* is something of a fraud, as the *Tao Tè Ching* was never declared an actual classic by the literati of China except for a brief period during the T'ang dynasty, who claimed descent from Lao Tzu. Instead, the title *Ching* was given by popular acclaim. The book was and is viewed as a classic by believers, and as such stands in a special honoured position within the Taoist Canon of Sacred Texts.

What happened to the book is what happened to Taoism itself. It was transformed from one amongst a number of competing schools of philosophy into a major new religion – albeit one infused with the spirit of the world's oldest religion, shamanism.

Taoism

It was in the first few centuries AD, then, that Taoism was first perceived as a salvationary faith offering hope to the millions of ordinary people in China. Through the rituals of confession and absolution it was possible, indeed is still possible, for the believer to be reintegrated into the flow of the natural world – a flow, a Tao, which affects both the physical and the spiritual worlds. For in Taoism as a belief system the old themes of shamanism, which had been increasingly marginalised, even vilified by the Confucians, re-emerged as a vital strand. A whole panoply of gods and goddesses arose, rituals of immense complexity were devised, and tens of thousands of sacred texts were 'revealed'. Yet through all this growth and transformation, an essential element has persisted which links this religion to the philosophy of the *Tao Te Ching*.

Central to Taoism as a faith is a sense of the balance of the universe, a sense that human activity must be in tune with the natural flows and rhythms of the universe – in other words with the Tao itself. Inherent within this is a belief in the twin forces of the universe, yin and yang. These two antagonistic forces must be kept in proper equilibrium, otherwise the world will tilt out of balance and all manner of disasters occur. This is what much of Taoist ritual is concerned with, what the different gods and goddesses are there for. They exist to protect, to reharmonise, to offer forgiveness or to be invoked to restore the balance. Through cosmic liturgies, and through rituals to do with everything from where your bed should be placed to the protection of the dead, Taoism seeks to restore or maintain the natural balance of the universe.

To be sure, much of this is well hidden behind the usual ephemera of popular religion, but if you want to understand the heart of Taoism as practised throughout the Chinese world read chapter 42 of the *Tao Te Ching*. It contains what could be called the fundamental creed of Taoism, and it is this understanding of the dynamics of existence that underpins all Taoist thought, action and belief.

Tao is the Mother of the Whole.

The

Whole

splits   into

Yin   and   Yang

From these two comes three,
from three comes all life.

The Tao Te Ching today

In modern Taoist affections, the *Tao Te Ching* holds a preeminent position, but it is not viewed in quite the way that one might expect. The text is studied, especially as a handbook to meditation, but more commonly as a handbook to ritual or even to magic. I have seen the text placed under the pillow of a man suffering from brain damage and on one occasion saw some pages from it burnt and the ashes mixed with water and given to a sick child. The book can also be used as a charm against evil forces and hung or placed near a doorway or in the vicinity where a ghost has been seen. However, the *Tao Te Ching* is not considered to be the best type of charm. These are usually ones written by later Taoist leaders, such as Chang Tao Ling who was active in the second century AD, who explicitly set out to exorcise ghosts.

Through the vast array of commentaries on the *Tao Te Ching* which are themselves treated as sacred texts, Taoism has turned this handbook of leadership and wisdom into a veritable gold mine of allegorical imagery, magical incantation and ritual symbolism. For example, one basic adaptation of its symbolism is to take all reference to the state, country, people, rulers and so forth as being images of the body. Thus the people become the limbs, the ruler becomes the head, and the state itself becomes the heart or the mind. The whole text is thus transformed either into a textbook of inner alchemy, transforming the body into an immortal body through meditation practices; or a handbook to external alchemy, a guidebook which supposedly assists you in literally changing your physical body into an immortal one through digesting certain materials – jade, gold and mercury being favourites!

Few people in China have ever read the *Tao Te Ching*; that is not its role in Chinese life. Sages, monks and those interested in philosophy will of course have read it. But it is not a text known by the vast majority of people, for it is not seen – except in its more magical or allegorical modes – to be relevant to them. They have usually encountered it as a hazy background text which lies behind a smokescreen of incense, incantation and ritual. Yet for all that, the core notion of the Tao rules and dominates their thinking.

I have been asked why, having done my own translation of the *Tao Te Ching* with Kwok Man Ho and Jay Ramsay, I should want to recommend and introduce another version. My answer is simple. When we did our translation, we worked from the Chinese and sought to rediscover its meaning and power as a Chinese classic which now speaks way beyond its cultural boundaries. But Timothy, in his rendering, has put across, from his own personal experience, a deep sense of the spiritual nourishment contained within the book. He has also approached it as one whose profession is to play with words and draw out of them their deepest meanings in our contemporary culture. His version of the *Tao Te Ching* is wonderfully crisp, almost brutally sharp and sparse in its use of language. Freed from any literalism, he has responded to the ideas. My task has been occasionally to rein in his enthusiasm and sometimes to draw him back to a more faithful following of the Chinese original. But what struck me the first time I read his work, and what has continued to strike me, is his ability to express, in contemporary English, the core ideas of ancient China – but without any of the 'Chinglish' which bedevils so many versions of Chinese texts.

In working on this text we have been most fortunate to have had the assistance, guidance and inspiration of the China Taoist Association. This is the official body representing all the major schools of Taoism in China today and it is based in the beautiful ancient White Cloud Temple,

Beijing. Here, surrounded by statues and paintings of Lao Tzu, teachers and scholars of Taoism have taken me through the text of the *Tao Te Ching*, drawing out its deeper meanings and significance. Any text, viewed through the eyes of believers, comes alive in a way which no amount of scholarship can make it do and my experiences with these men and women helped to reinforce my impression of the *Tao* as a living text.

The life of the *Tao Te Ching* lies in providing a handbook or guidebook to living. Here, distilled in these extraordinary eighty-one chapters are insights and wisdom which have stood the test of time. Drawing upon one of the oldest, continuous cultures in the world, its poetic and yet at times precise guidance offers a fascinating vision of the continuity of life. Written over 2300 years ago, its sharpness, its incisiveness and its expressiveness speak as clearly today as they have done down the centuries. At times I feel as if there has been a straight leap from the pen of the Chinese editor living 300 years before Christ, to the computer of Timothy, living at the end of the second millennium AD. For this is perennial wisdom which addresses the nature of the human condition. In so doing it speaks both as straightforward advice and as inspired revelation, yet it makes no presumptions about the Divine, or gods, or God or even spirituality. Instead it opens us up and helps us hear the flow and rush of the Tao in ourselves and in those around us and within our world.

Martin Palmer
Series Editor

A New Version of the Tao Te Ching

德

Tao is not something ancient or Chinese. Tao is here and now. The fragments of poetry, philosophy, paradox and politics that make up this book are not only of relevance to some abstract understanding of the oriental mind in past millennia, but also impact concretely on our own strange lives.

Although written in a different age, in a foreign language and in an alien culture, the *Tao Te Ching* addresses an unchanging mystery. My aim in this rendering has been to unearth the universal voice of common human experience from beneath the cultural rubble that has covered it during two and a half thousand years of history; to allow the text to convey its wonder as directly to you, here and now, as it did to its original readers in their own here and now.

I have, therefore, avoided the kind of vocabulary that I feel may alienate a modern reader. For example, most translations use the word 'sage', or something similar. If we lived in a culture like that of modern India, where gurus or spiritual masters are a common part of life, this would be meaningful; but to Western ears, I feel this sounds exotic and remote. Likewise 'virtue' as a translation for *Te* sounds too moralistic and old-fashioned. I have used 'Natural Goodness', which gives a sense that *Te* comes naturally from following Tao. It is not a moral code – it is the underlying goodness of the universe.

Archaic words like 'chariot' sound historical and irrelevant to us. I have updated them with terms like 'car', which have the same familiarity to modern ears as these archaic words would have had to the original readers. In a sense, this approach presents a more 'accurate' representation of the original meaning than a literal word-for-word translation.

Apart from 'Tao', which is now in common usage, I have avoided all Chinese transliterations. With difficult concepts like *Wu Wei* I have used different phrases, as appropriate: for example 'doing by just being'. The usual translation, 'non-action', is misleading. It sounds totally passive. My practice of Tai Chi Chuan has led me to understand that *Wu Wei* is both Yin and Yang – both passive and active. More like adjusting a sail to harness a prevailing wind than 'going with the flow' like a dead fish!

The form of this rendering has been important to me. I have sought to embrace the principles of economy and spaciousness that the text extols. I have centred the lines to give a visual sense of fluidity and balance within movement. It also has a slight echo of the Chinese language about it – reading downwards – which I like. The end result has been these shapes on the page which have come to fascinate me. In places I have created a type of word-picture to illustrate the particular meaning of a stanza. As Chinese characters come originally from pictograms, this does not seem an unjustified liberty.

My rendering has been informed throughout by the conviction that the inexpressible mystery that the mythic Lao Tzu is gesturing towards in this extraordinary work is the same mystery that I, in my own small way, have encountered during my brief life-journey; and the same that the great masters of this century have known and tried to convey to us – each from their own unique tradition and personal perspective. People like Sri Nisargadatta, Ramana Maharishi and Suzuki Roshi. The politics of the *Tao Te Ching* often reminds me of Mahatma Gandhi, whose 'Satyagraha' or 'Truth-force' resonates with *Te* – chapter 80 is like the description of a Gandhian utopia! It is by holding this ancient text in the light shone by contemporary teachers that I have been able to make out its perennial wisdom.

I am not a Chinese scholar. My method has been to meditate upon many different, often divergent, translations of a chapter, until it began to speak to me in a direct and simple way. I have been fortunate enough to have Martin Palmer as my editor in this endeavour. Unlike myself, he is an expert in the Chinese language, and so has been able to help me return to the original Chinese when my rendering has wandered and encourage me when I have legitimately dared to explore unconventional territory.

Lao Tzu says that he is not difficult to understand, so I have taken him at his word! My assumption has been that whilst the text is often paradoxical and sometimes obscure, it is not inconsistent or esoteric. My meditations have all endeavoured to tease out the obvious from the abstruse.

Passing such intense and intimate time with this mysterious old masterpiece has been an extraordinary experience. I found myself feeling as if I was staring into a great and empty void – and at the same time being held and nurtured by the most caring of mothers. Paradoxes like this are at the heart of knowing Tao. Being able to stretch wide enough to embrace the two poles of an apparent contradiction is the secret to understanding the mystery of the 'Whole', which contains them both. Tao is uniquely Chinese – yet it is universal. It is ancient – yet it is timeless. It is only ever 'now-here' – and so it is 'nowhere'.

Timothy Freke

1

Tao is not a way that can be pointed out.
Nor an idea that can be defined.

Tao is indefinable original totality.
Ideas create the appearance of separate things.

Always hidden, it is the mysterious essence.
Always manifest, it is the outer appearances.

Essence and appearance are the same.
Only ideas make them seem separate.
Mystified?

Tao is mystery.
This is the gateway to understanding.

2

Something can be beautiful, if something else is ugly.
Someone can be good, if someone else is bad.

Presence and absence.
Short and long.
High and low.
Before and after.
Gibberish and meaning.
They can only exist together!

So,
the Wise can act, by just being,
and teach without speaking.
Things come to them, because they let them go.
They create by not trying to possess.
They succeed by not seeking reward.
What needs to be done is done – and then forgotten.
They are always moving on.

3

The Wise don't make themselves out to be special,
so no one competes with them.

They don't accumulate riches,
so no one steals from them.

They govern by example,
so no one is misled.

They aren't controlled by desire,
so they don't cause confusion.

They're not greedy for food or power,
and so they are full of well-being.

People don't understand what they do,
but no one wants to take over.

4

Tao is like an empty space,
that can never be filled up.
Yet it contains everything:
Blunt and sharp,
resolved and confused,
bright and dull,
the whole of Creation.

Hidden, but always present.
Who created it?
It existed before the Creator.

5

Heaven and Earth don't have human feelings.
To them all things are like idols:
Sacred – but also just empty forms.
In the same way the Wise honour everyone,
knowing they are nothing.

Heaven and Earth are like two handles of a bellows,
that push together and pull apart,
forever creating Life.

Why waste breath trying to comprehend this?
Better to know the Source, where they meet.

6

Emptiness is eternal.
The Mother of all Life.

The primal source.

She is dimly visible,
as if behind a veil.

Be empty,
and you will never be drained.

7

Heaven and Earth go on forever.
Why?
Because they have no sense of self.

The Wise advance,
by holding back.

They lose themselves,
and find the Whole.

Fulfilment comes from selflessness.

8

Great goodness is like water.
It flows everywhere, filling everything.
It is life-giving, by its very nature.
It humbly settles in the lowest places,
like someone who follows Tao.

Make your heart like a lake,
with a calm, still surface,
and great depths of kindness.

Nurture your true nature.
Make love your gift to others.
Only talk the truth.

Flow around obstacles, don't confront them.
Don't struggle to succeed.
Wait for the right moment.

No need for strife – no need for blame.

9

Fill a bowl to the brim and it will spill.
Make a blade too sharp and it will soon blunt.

Amass too much wealth and you will never protect it.
Too much success breeds arrogance,
and arrogance brings downfall.

When enough has been done – time to stop!
This is Heaven's Way.

10

Can you value your uniqueness, as part of the Whole?
Be subtle as breath, and supple as a baby?
Be a polished mirror, reflecting Truth perfectly?

Can you love and lead people, without recourse to dogma?
Temper the 'Masculine' and enhance the 'Feminine'?

Can you be open and receiving in every way?
Birthing and nourishing, but not possessing.
Helping, but not seeking gratitude.
Guiding, but not controlling.
This is
Natural Goodness.

11

A wheel is useful,
because of the hole at the centre of the hub.

A clay pot is useful,
because it contains empty space.

Doors and windows are useful,
because they are gaps in the walls.

The value of what is there,
lies in what is not there!

12

Colour
may blind the eyes.

Sound
may deafen the ears.

Taste
may dull the palate.

Desire
may trouble the heart.

Excitement
may confuse the mind.

The Wise don't put their trust in how things seem.
They follow gut feelings.

This is their choice.

13

Success causes fear as much as failure does.

Believing you are your personality,
is the source of all your troubles.

What does it mean,
'Success causes fear as much as failure does'?
Well, when you achieve success,
you become frightened of losing it.
That's what it means.

What does it mean,
'Believing you are your personality,
is the source of all your troubles'?
The reason you experience troubles
is because you think you are just a persona.
If you saw through this – you'd have no problems.

Stop clinging to your personality,
and see all beings as yourself.
Such a person could be trusted with the whole world.

14

You can't see it, because it has no form.
You can't hear it, because it makes no noise.
You can't touch it, because it has no substance.
It cannot be known in these ways,
because it is the all-embracing Whole.
It is not high and light,
or low and dark.
Indefinable yet continually present.
It is nothing at all.
It is the formless form.
The imageless image.
It can't be grasped by the imagination.
It has no beginning and no end.

This is the essence of Tao.
Stay in harmony with this ancient presence,
and you will know the fullness of each present moment.

15

The Ancient Masters understood Mystery.
The depths of their wisdom was unfathomable,
so all we have are descriptions of how they looked....

Careful, as if crossing a frozen river.
Alert, as if aware of danger.
Respectful, like a guest.
Yielding, like melting ice.
Simple, like uncarved wood.
Empty, like a valley.

Trying to understand
is like straining to see through muddy water.
Be still, and allow the mud to settle.
Remain still, until it is time to act.

Those who follow Tao don't seek to arrive anywhere,
so their journey is never over.

16

Be empty – be still.
Watch everything just come and go.
Emerging from the Source – returning to the Source.
This is the way of Nature.

Be at peace.
Be aware of the Source.
This is the fulfilment of your destiny.
Know that which never changes.
This is enlightenment.

Without this awareness,
you are stumbling blindly.
With this awareness,
you can embrace everything.

Embrace everything,
and you will be equanimous.
Be equanimous,
and you can truly serve.
Truly serve,
and you will be filled with Spirit.
Filled with Spirit,
you will be one with Tao.
One with Tao,
you will know the eternal,
and need never fear you will cease to exist,
even when your body has turned to dust.

17

Great Leaders are hardly noticed.
The Wise are loved and praised.

Dictators are feared.
Hypocrites are despised.

The Wise promise nothing,
and so they are trusted.

When success is achieved without too much direction,
everyone says: 'It just happened!'

18

When people lose touch with Tao,
questions of moral duty arise.

When intelligence and cleverness are overvalued,
people start the great pretence.

When natural affection does not flow,
questions of family loyalty arise.

When a nation is confused,
it is prey to patriotic leaders.

19

'Give up trying to seem holy,
forget trying to appear wise,
and it will be a lot better for everyone.'

'Abandon trying to seem good,
throw out self-righteousness,
and rediscover natural compassion.'

'Stop trying to be so smart,
quit being calculating,
and you won't become a rogue.'

These three sayings are important,
but I want to add this....
Be simple
and true to your own nature.
Be selfless
and at peace with the way things are.

20

You'll find your life easier,
if you stop trying to seem so clever!
'Yes or No?' ... who cares?
'Bad or Good?' ... who knows?

I feel fear, just like everybody else.
But while other people are only happy
walking in the spring sunshine,
on the lookout for fame and gain,
I am content to be alone and drifting,
with no interest in my fortunes
– like a baby too young to smile.

Everyone else has more than enough.
What do I care?
I'm a fool.
Confused and muddled.
Others are bright and sharp as a knife.
What do I know?
I am blunt and weak.

I am surrounded by a great sea of people,
always on the move.
While I am like a restless wind,
drifting without direction.
Everyone else is busy.
I am aimless like a passing beggar.

Sometimes I feel so different to other people.
But I always know I am a child nourished by the Mother.

21

Natural Goodness only flows from following Tao.

Tao

Elusive and mysterious – yet expressed in form.

Elusive and mysterious – the seed of creation.

It is real.

See for yourself.

From the beginning of time – until this present moment,

Tao

is eternally creating Creation.

How do I know the nature of things?

Because I know Tao.

22

Give up, and you will succeed.

Bow, and you will stand tall.

Be empty, and you will be filled.

Let go of the old, and let in the new.

Have little, and there is room to receive more.

The wise stand out,

because they see themselves as part of the Whole.

They shine,

because they don't want to impress.

They achieve great things,

because they don't look for recognition.

Their wisdom is contained in what they are,

not their opinions.

They refuse to argue,

so no one argues with them.

The Ancients said: 'Give up and you will succeed.'

Is this empty nonsense?

Try it.

If you are sincere, you will find fulfilment.

23

It is natural, when you've something to say,
to be direct and use few words;
like a whirlwind which passes quickly,
or a rainstorm which is soon spent.
Heaven and Earth create whirlwinds and rainstorms,
and they don't last for long.
Likewise a person should be brief and to the point.

Follow Tao and become Tao.
Follow Natural Goodness and become naturally good.
Abandon either of these and you will feel abandoned.

Seek Tao and it finds you.
Hold to Natural Goodness and it will never desert you.
Lose either of these and you will be lost.

If you do not trust,
you will not find what is trustworthy.

24

Those who stand on tiptoe are unsteady.
Those who take large strides, tire quickly.
Those who think they know, never learn.
Those who want to stand out, don't value others.
Those who are self-important are never respected.

These ways are like unnecessary baggage,
or food left over after a feast.
To the followers of Tao, they have no use.

25

Mysteriously existing before Heaven and Earth.
Silent and empty.
An unchanging oneness.
An everchanging presence.
The Mother of all Life.

It is impossible to really give it a name,
but I call it 'Tao'.
Without wishing to define it,
it could be called 'The Whole'.
The Whole moves as if in a circle:
Turning away and returning to itself.

Tao is the Whole.
The Whole contains the universe.
The Universe contains the Earth.
The Earth contains Humankind.
These are the four great elements of creation.

Humankind follows the ways of the Earth.
The Earth follows the ways of the Universe.
The Universe follows the ways of Tao.
Tao follows its own nature.

26

Light things need heavy roots.
Moving things need still centres.

The Wise go through each day,
without losing sight of what is important to them.
Although they may see many desirable things,
they don't get distracted.

Why are our leaders so often political lightweights?
Because they are distracted and have lost their roots.
They are restless and have lost their still centre.

27

The Wise don't leave tracks for others to follow,
or speak to convince their listener.
They don't calculate their own profit.
They can close their door securely, without locks.
They can bind things tightly, without knots.

They care for everyone and reject no one.
Care for everything and reject nothing.
This is what it means to be 'enlightened'.

A good person is a role model for a bad person,
because everyone has the potential for goodness.
If this example is not followed,
or this potential not nurtured,
confusion follows,
however clever people think they are.

This is the heart of the matter.

28

To be filled with the masculine power of Yang,
follow the feminine nature of Yin.
Be empty like a valley,
where water gathers to form a stream.
Gather Natural Goodness,
until you are like a little child again.

To be filled with light,
acknowledge what is dark.
Be an example to the world.
Allow the stream of Natural Goodness
to carry you back to the Infinite.

To be filled with honour,
be humble about your shortcomings.
Be empty as a valley.
Follow the flow of Natural Goodness,
to the sea of Primal Simplicity.

The Wise are aware of the Whole,
while interacting with the parts.
This is how they can help without harming.

29

If you try to rule the world, you'll ruin it.
The world is sacred.
It's not private property in need of refurbishment!
If you try to shape it to fit your ideas,
you will destroy it.
If you try to understand it,
once and for all,
it will seem incomprehensible.

3 0

If you ever advise a leader about Tao,
tell them not to use force,
because what you do – comes back to you.

Weeds grow where armies have camped.
Wars lead to famine.

Do what has to be done,
but don't abuse power.

Get things done,
but don't make a show.

Get things done,
but don't boast.

Get things done,
but don't be smug.

Get things done,
because it has to be that way.

Get things done,
but not by force.

To use force is to be weak.
This is not Tao.
This is not the way to have a lasting effect.

31

An advisor who follows Tao never counsels force.
The Wise go the way of peace.
The war-mongers go the way of conflict.
Weapons are embodiments of fear.
The Wise use them only when they have no choice.
To them, peace is the greatest good,
and victory in war, no cause for celebration.
If you can rejoice about slaughter,
then celebrate victory.
But if you can rejoice about slaughter,
you have lost the Way.
In happy times the peace-makers are honoured.
In sad times people are distinguished in battle.
The commanders of an army should conduct war,
as if it were a funeral.
Many people are being killed,
so grief and mourning are appropriate.
Let a victory celebration be like a memorial service.

3 2

Tao can never be conceptualised.
It is so simple, it seems irrelevant.
But,
if leaders could live by it,
everything would unfold as they wished.
Gentle rain would unite Heaven and Earth.
People would find their place,
without being ordered about.

Ideas divide up the Whole.
Enough ideas!
Time to stop and avoid yet more problems.

Following Tao in the world
is like being a mountain stream,
that becomes part of a valley brook,
that becomes part of a great river,
that flows to the sea.

33

Wisdom is seeing the true nature of others.
Enlightenment is seeing the true nature of Tao.

Mastering others requires force.
Mastering yourself requires strength.

Being self-sufficient,
is being truly rich.

Have the will to do what has to be done.
Have the endurance to stay where you need to be.

To die, while living,
is to be in the eternal present.

34

The Great Tao is everywhere,
to the right and to the left.
Everything depends on it,
but it requires nothing back.
It does its work without seeking reward.
It feeds and clothes everyone,
but doesn't want to be their master.

It has no aims. It is very small.
It nurtures all things without them knowing.
It is very great.

It is the same with the Wise.
They don't try to appear great,
and so are truly great.

35

Everyone is attracted to a person who knows Tao,
because they are peaceful and happy.

A traveller may stop for nice food and good music,
but a description of Tao seems bland and tasteless.
It looks like nothing special.
It sounds like nothing special.
But live by it, and you will never tire of it.

36

The expanded will eventually shrink.
The strong will eventually weaken.

The high and mighty will eventually fall.
The rich will eventually be ruined.

Because this is the way things work,
softness and weakness can overcome hardness and strength.

A fish is safe, just by staying in deep waters.
So, a country can be safe without displaying weapons.

37

Tao just is, and everything gets done.
If leaders could be this way,
people would change by themselves.
If people were compelled by desire,
their leaders would lead them back
to their original simplicity.
Eventually there would be no desire,
and without desire there is peace.
In this way the world rights itself.

38

A 'do-gooder' wants to be seen to be good.
Natural Goodness is unconcerned with appearances.
A 'do-gooder' may be endlessly busy,
but there always seems more to be done.
Natural Goodness seems to do nothing,
and good things just happen.

Kind people act
without thought of themselves.
Just people act
according to a set of ideas.
Moralisers act
and if people don't go along with them,
they raise their fists,
ready to enforce their point of view!

When Tao is lost,
there is still Natural Goodness.
When Natural Goodness is lost,
there is still kindness.
When kindness is lost,
there is still justice.
When justice is lost,
there are only social niceties,
and these are not genuine or honest.
Then all is lost.

Thinking you know what should happen,
can seem like the flowering of Tao,
but it will make a fool of you.
The Wise stay with what is.
This is the fruit of Tao.
They choose the fruit, not the flower.

39

From ancient times,
the nature of the Whole has been observable in its parts:
The clear heavens and the firm earth,
potent spirits and fertile valleys,
all living beings and all great leaders.
They are as they are,
because they are part of the Whole.
If this were not so,
the heavens would fall and the earth would split,
the spirits would be impotent
and the valleys would dry up,
everything would die
and leaders would certainly fall.

Honour is rooted in humility.

The high has its foundations in the low.

Most people hate to be lonely, orphaned or unimportant.

But Great Leaders see themselves as unimportant,

and embrace the unfortunate as part of themselves.

This is to be rooted in humility – don't you think?

They know success is not an advantage.

They don't desire to glitter like jewellery.

They are as ordinary as stone.

Gain by losing or lose by gaining.

I'm just saying what others have said before me:

'Live a violent life, and you will die a violent death.'

This is the heart of my teachings.

40

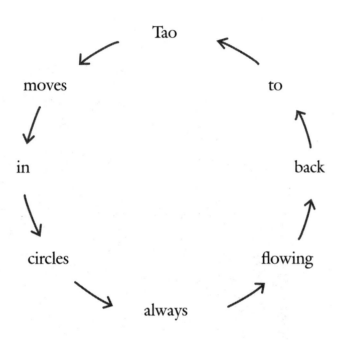

Tao is ever yielding – constantly creating,

every thing from no thing.

41

On hearing about Tao –
wise students consistently practise what they learn;
average students give it a thought now and then;
foolish students think it's all ridiculous.
But Tao would not be Tao, if no one poked fun!

So, there are these sayings:
'Tao is clear, but seems dark.
Tao goes forward, but seems to retreat.
Tao is easy, but seems to be hard.
Natural Goodness seems empty.
Great purity seems imperfect.
Goodness is abundant, but seems insufficient.
Goodness is strong, but seems frail.
Goodness is evident, but seems hidden.
A perfect square actually has no corners.
A great work is never completed.
The highest notes cannot be heard.
The greatest form has no shape.'

Tao is not revealed by ideas. Tao exists beyond concepts.
Yet it is true to say that
everything is nourished and fulfilled,
only by Tao.

42

Tao is Mother of the Whole.

The
Whole

splits   into

Yin   and   Yang

From these two comes three;
from three comes all life.

Yin is form, the container.
Yang is essence, the contained.
Like the in-breath and the out-breath of Life,
these two are one.

43

Strength is tamed by gentleness,
like a rider controlling a galloping horse.

Water seeps through, even though there are no cracks.
This is how I know the value of just being.

Very few in this world can learn from silence,
or act by just being.

44

Which matters more,
what you are or how you seem?

Which is worth more,
what you are or what you have?

Which causes most suffering,
loss or gain?

If you don't work too hard,
you won't wear yourself out.

If you don't hoard too much,
you won't suffer great losses.

If you don't want too much,
you won't be discontent.

Knowing when to stop avoids unnecessary problems,
and helps you keep going.

4 5

The greatest achievement seems like falling short,
but its effects are beyond measure.
Being filled up feels like being emptied out,
but never like running dry.

Straightforwardness seems obscure.
Great skill seems clumsy.
Great intelligence looks foolish.
Great eloquence sounds like blathering.

Be calm, not cold – be calm, not hot.
Tranquil and equanimous – see order within chaos.

46

In a country where Tao is understood, there are carthorses.
In a country where Tao is ignored, there are warhorses.

The greatest mistake is to be ruled by desire.
The greatest curse is to be discontent.

Getting what you want may be the greatest misfortune.
Appreciate what you have and you will always have enough.

47

You can know everything – without going anywhere.

You don't see the Way of Heaven,
by staring out the window.

The more you go looking – the less you will find.

The Wise know,
there is nowhere to go.

They see by not looking – they act by just being.

48

Someone seeking learning, knows more and more.
Someone seeking Tao, knows less and less.
Less and less, until
things just
are what
they
are

By simply being,
everything gets done.

Get things done,
by letting them happen.

Struggling all the time,
gets you nowhere.

49

A wise heart is big enough to embrace everyone.

I am good to the good and I am good to the bad,
because it is good to be good.
I trust the trustworthy and I trust the untrustworthy,
because I trust in trust.

The Wise are not full of themselves.
They are careful not to push others away.
They teach how to live well, by their example.
They treat everyone as family.

50

At a crossroads,

where one way leads to Life – and one way leads to Death,

three out of ten choose the way to Life;

three out of ten choose the way to Death;

three out of ten want to go the way to Life,

but drift off down the road to Death.

Why?

Because they are wrapped up in superficialities.

I have heard it said –

Those who know how to live well, travel without danger.

Living a good life is like being protected,

and living a bad life is as if under attack!

The Enlightened are invulnerable,

No horn can gore them.

No claw can tear them.

No weapon can pierce them.

Death cannot touch those who truly know how to live.

51

Tao gives life to all living things,
and its Natural Goodness nurtures them.
It forms them according to their unique nature,
in relationship with their environment.
This is why it is natural for everything
to spontaneously honour Tao and its Natural Goodness.

Tao gives life to all living things,
and its Natural Goodness
nourishes,
tends,
comforts,
feeds,
shelters
and protects them.

Tao works mysteriously.
Giving life, but then letting go.
Accomplishing its purpose without controlling.
Guiding not forcing.

52

In the beginning the Mother gave birth to everything.
If you know the Mother, you know you are her child.
Remember your Mother,
and you will lose your fear of death.

Shut your mouth,
close your door on the world,
and you will always know the fullness of life.
Open your mouth,
get wrapped up in busyness,
and you'll never get the help you need.

Pay attention to the little things.
Make yielding your strength.
Don't go looking for trouble.
Follow your light and refind your original clarity.
Always do this.

53

If I've got any sense, I'll just follow the road of Tao,
and my only fear will be of getting sidetracked.
The road is easy enough to follow,
but people wander off everywhere....

Leaders live in big houses,
while the fields are full of weeds.
The granaries are empty,
while the rich wear the latest fashion.
People carry weapons and eat and drink to excess.
Their riches are stolen from the poor.
They are arrogant thieves.

This is certainly not Tao!

54

What is well planted, cannot be uprooted.
What is firmly grasped, doesn't slip away.

Nurture Natural Goodness within yourself,
and you will feel its benefits.
Make it part of the family,
and it will grow from generation to generation.
Make it the centre of your community,
and it will flourish.
Make it the leader of your nation,
and it will be abundant.
Make it the whole of your world,
and whichever way you turn,
you will meet Natural Goodness.

Embrace others as part of yourself.
Treat every family as your family.
See all communities as your community.
Think of nations everywhere as your nation.
Know that your world is everyone's world.

Why do I see things this way?
Because this is the way things are.

55

If you want to know about Natural Goodness,
take a look at little babies.
They are so innocent,
it seems impossible to think of them coming to harm.
Their bones are soft and their muscles weak,
but their grip is firm.
They are whole in themselves,
without union with their opposite sex.
They can cry all day and still not get hoarse!
They are completely in harmony.

To be in harmony, is to know that which never changes.
To know the changeless, is enlightenment.
Struggling to achieve enlightenment is crazy!
Trying to control the Life-Energy will exhaust you.
Forcing growth, hastens death.
This is not Tao.

56

Those who know, don't push it on others.
Those who claim to know, probably don't.

Shut up!
Go inside!
Soften your sharp edges.
Simplify your thoughts.
Follow your own light.
Be ordinary.
Then you will see for yourself,
that you are part of the Whole.

Whether faced with friend or enemy,
loss or gain,
fame or shame,
the Wise remain equanimous.
This is what makes them so extraordinary.

5 7

Holding to the letter of the law,
may be appropriate to keep a country in order.
Using surprise tactics,
may be appropriate to win a war.
But only acting from your true being,
is always appropriate.

What makes me say this?
I'll tell you.
The more shoulds and shouldn'ts there are,
the poorer the quality of life.
The more powerful weapons become,
the more destruction there will be.
The more ingenious people get,
the more dangerous what they create.
The more laws there are,
the more people break them.

The Wise say:

'If I practise just being,

then others may change themselves.

If I am at peace, then others may become peaceful.

If I don't get in the way, everyone will be richer.

If I am empty of desires,

others may return to being simple

and simply being.'

5 8

If a country is ruled in an unobtrusive way,
its people will be honest and live simply.
But if government is invasive,
people become devious or apathetic.

Bad things lead to good things.
Good things lead to bad things.
Who knows how the future will turn out?
Is there a right way?
What now is normal will soon seem strange.
Those trying to do good, end up doing harm.
And so it goes on.
Everyone is caught up in it.

That is why the Wise set an example without criticising.
They are honest, but not hurtful.
Straightforward, but not intolerant.
They shine their light,
but not so brightly that it blinds.

5 9

When being of service or caring for others,
don't overdo it.
Meaning – let go of your ideas about how it should be.

Natural Goodness is like a deep well inside of you.
If you have been drawing from this well,
then nothing is impossible.
There are no limits to what you can achieve,
and you are able to truly help.

Be like a mother,
and the effects of what you do will last.
Have deep roots in Tao.
See the eternal beyond the impermanent.

60

Cooking a small fish and ruling a big country,
need equal care.

When the world is ruled by Tao, Evil is powerless.
Not that it doesn't exist.
It just has no power to harm people.

The Wise don't want anyone to come to harm.

When people don't hurt each other,
Natural Goodness spreads throughout the land.

61

Rivers naturally flow to lowlands and unite.
A great country, like low land, draws everything to it,
in the way that a woman can attract a man,
without needing to do anything.
This is the power of passivity.

So,
if a big country respects a small country,
it will win the trust of the small country.
If a small country respects a big country,
it will win the trust of the big country.
A country which is small is already humble,
but a country which is big has to make itself humble.
A big country wants to expand,
and a small country wants protection.
They both get what they want,
when the big country humbles itself.

62

Tao is home for all creation.
A treasure to the good.
A refuge for the bad.
It makes true words, priceless.
Good deeds, the perfect gift.
It doesn't abandon someone because they are lost.

So,
when a leader is sworn in or a government takes office,
don't send valuable gifts and fancy cars.
Be still,
and offer Tao.

The Ancients, who valued Tao so highly, said:
'With Tao there can be no mistakes.'

To know Tao
is the most wonderful thing in the world.

6 3

Strive not to struggle – achieve by just being.
Savour the flavourless – value the unimportant.
Meet unkindness with compassion.

Tackle difficult jobs while they are still easy,
and big jobs while they are small.
The troubles of the world can only be solved
before they get out of hand.
The great affairs of the world can only be sorted out,
by paying attention to all the small things.

The Wise don't attempt anything great,
and so achieve great things.
Someone who promises the world,
will never live up to their promise.
Someone who thinks everything is easy,
will inevitably find things hard.
The Wise don't avoid difficulties,
so nothing remains difficult.

64

When at peace, remember danger.

When things are easy, don't get complacent

Brittle things are easily shattered.

Small things are easily lost.

Set things right before they go wrong.

Get things sorted before they get confused.

A mighty tree grows from a tiny shoot.

A tower block nine storeys high,

starts as a heap of earth.

A thousand mile journey begins with one step.

Struggle and you'll ruin it.

Grasp and you'll lose it.

The Wise don't struggle – so nothing gets spoilt.

The Wise don't grasp – so they lose nothing.

People usually mess things up,

just as they are about to succeed.

Be as careful at the completion,

as you were at the start.

Advance and retreat,

hard and easy,

strength and weakness,

victim and victor,

the Wise remain equanimous in the midst of

extremes and excesses.

They desire to be without desires.

They don't go after precious things,

just because they're hard to get.

They study what others ignore.

They bring people's attention to what has been overlooked.

They help everything find its true nature,

and would not presume to do any more than this.

65

The Ancients who knew Tao,
didn't try to explain it to everyone else.
They let people be simple.
People who are filled with ideas are difficult to lead well.

Leaders who rely on ideas confuse the country.
Leaders who avoid ideas are a blessing to the country.
Understand the difference between these two ways,
and choose to be an example of Natural Goodness.

Natural Goodness is so deep and far-reaching,
it leads everything back to an awareness of the Whole.

66

Streams and rivers flow to the sea,
because it lies below them.
That's why it is the greatest body of water.

Following this example –
If the Wise want to guide, they are humble.
If they want to lead, they work from behind.
In this way,
people don't feel pushed about.

The Wise lead without obstructing.
Everyone helps them without resentment.
Because they won't compete,
no one can compete with them.

6 7

People say that my talk of Tao is all well and good,
but it doesn't relate to anything!
But this is precisely what makes it so important.
Tao doesn't 'relate' to anything,
because Tao 'is' everything!

I have three qualities that I treasure and hold close:
Love,
simplicity,
and daring not to put myself before others.
From love comes courage.
From simplicity comes generosity.
From daring not to be first, comes leadership.
People today want to be generous, but not because of love.
They want to be generous, but not through simplicity.
They want to lead, but not with humility.
This is hopeless.

In conflict, it is love that wins.
Love is the strongest protection.
If you have love,
it is as if Heaven itself were keeping you safe.

68

A good guide doesn't insist.
A good employer doesn't push people around.
A good competitor isn't angry,
and if they win, they aren't vindictive.

Natural Goodness doesn't struggle,
it brings out the best in people.
In ancient times this was called 'Heaven's Way'.

69

There is a saying concerning strategy:

'Don't invite a fight, but face it if you have to.
Better to retreat a foot than advance an inch.'

This is making your move, while staying still.
Rolling up your sleeves, but not clenching your fists.
Having an adversary, but not an enemy.
Being armed, but not with weapons.

It is a big mistake not to respect an adversary.
If I did that, I'd have already lost what I value most.

Only the compassionate truly win.

70

It is easy to understand what I'm saying,
    but it seems like nobody does.
    It is easy to live by my teachings,
    but it seems like nobody wants to.

What I say and do is nothing new.
Understand that or you'll never understand me.

Although I am so rarely understood,
    it doesn't diminish the value of what I have.
    The Wise may look poor on the outside,
    because they keep their riches in their hearts.

71

It is healthy to know you know nothing.
Pretending to know is a kind of sickness.
Realising you are ill,
is the beginning of healing.
The Wise are sick of sickness,
and so they are well.

72

When people lack a sense of awe,
something aweful happens.

Don't intrude on people's private life,
or get in the way of them making a living.
Don't push them around,
and they won't end up resenting you.

Wisdom is knowing yourself,
but not having to make a show of it.
Having self-respect,
and not needing to seek approval.
Choosing what is within,
not what is without.

73

Daring to do and die

is to be courageous in the outer world.

Daring to be and live

is to act courageously in the inner world.

Both can help – both can harm.

Why?

Even the Wise have to admit they haven't got a clue.

Follow the Way of Heaven,

and you will succeed without struggling.

You will know the answer,

without asking the question.

All you need will come to you,

without being demanded.

You will be fulfilled without knowing desire.

The Way of Heaven is like a vast net,

although its mesh seems wide, it catches everything.

74

If people aren't afraid of death,
it's no good threatening to kill them.
But if people are frightened of dying,
then the death penalty might stop them breaking the law.
But,
there is already a supreme executioner
in charge of doing the killing.
If you put yourself in his place,
you are wielding the axe of a skilled woodsman,
and will end up injuring yourself.

7 5

Why are people hungry?
Because the rich take too much from them.
This is why they don't have enough.

Why are people rebellious?
Because the powerful push them around.
This is why they're angry.

Why do people risk death?
Because their leaders are sucking the life out of them.
They have so little to lose.

But even those with a little,
still have Life.

76

When you were born, you were soft and supple.
When you die, you will be hard and stiff.

Green shoots are fresh and full of vitality.
Dead plants are withered and dry.

Hard and stiff go with death.
Soft and supple go with life.

An inflexible army never wins a war.
A rigid tree is ready for the axe.

The hard and stiff falls,
and the soft and supple rises.

77

Following the Way of Heaven is like being an archer.
Aim
not too high – not too low.
Stress the string
not too little – not too much.

It is Heaven's Way to take from that which has too much,
and give to that which has too little.
This is not the way people do things.
They take from those with too little,
and give to those who already have too much.

Who has so much, he can offer it to everyone?
Only the person who knows Tao.
So,
the Wise do their work without seeking recognition.
They don't want the credit for their achievements.
They don't need to be important.

78

Nothing wears away hard strong rocks,
as well as soft weak water.

From this anyone can see
that softness is harder than hardness,
and weakness is stronger than strength.
But no one lives accordingly.

That is why the Ancients said:
'Embrace being a nobody,
and you are fit to be somebody.
Embrace the problems of ordinary life
and you will master the whole cosmos.

The Truth is paradoxical.

79

After an attempt at reconciliation,
if bitterness still remains – what then?
Meet bitterness with kindness.

The Wise act well, without demanding others do.
Someone who ignores Natural Goodness,
is always concerned that they are properly honoured.
Someone who knows Natural Goodness
honours their side of a relationship, regardless.

Heaven's Way
is never to favour this person over that person,
but always to be on the side of the Good.

80

Imagine a small country with few people.
It has powerful machines,
but no use for them.
The inhabitants respect death,
and don't take unnecessary risks.
There are ships and cars,
but no one travels in them.
There are tanks and guns,
but they are never paraded.
They turn their backs on sophistication,
and return to the simple ways.
Their food is wholesome.
Their clothes are simple.
Their homes are comfortable.
Their customs are delightful.
And although the neighbouring country is so near,
that they can hear each other's cocks crowing
and dogs barking,
they leave each other in peace to grow old and die.

81

The Truth may not sound convincing.

An eloquent speech may not be true.

Good people don't use the power of persuasion.

Those that argue aren't good.

You can be wise without being clever.

You can be clever without ever being wise.

The Wise aren't full of themselves.

The more they do for others – the more they feel fulfilled.

The more they give to others – the more they feel they have.

Heaven's Way

is to help without harming.

So,

the Wise act from their deepest being,

and without striving

bring everything to fulfilment.

Bibliography

Confucius, *The Analects*, Penguin Classics, 1979

Kwok, Palmer and Ramsey, *The Illustrated Tao Te Ching*, Element, 1993

Palmer, Martin, *The Elements of Taoism*, Element, 1991

Palmer, Ramsey and Zhao, *I Ching: The Shamanic Oracle of Change*, Thorsons, 1995

Shoo King (Shu Ching): The Great Plan, translated by James Legge, *The Chinese Classics*, Oxford University Press, 1871, vol. III; reprinted by Southern Material Center Inc, Taipai, 1983

Ssu-Ma Ch'ien, *Selections from the Records of the Historian*, translated by Yang Hsien-yi and Gladys Yang, Foreign Languages Press, Beijing, 1979, p. 167

About the Editors

Timothy Freke is a composer, author and teacher of Tai Chi Chuan and meditation.

Martin Palmer is a leading expert on Chinese literature and culture. He is director of ICOREC, the International Consultancy on Religion, Education and Culture based in Manchester. Martin is the author of many books on Chinese beliefs and world religions.